A FEELING *of* FULLNESS

Insights of a Divinely Guided   Journey Beyond Breast Cancer

WILHELMINA GRANT

To order additional copies of this book, contact:
Xlibris
1-888-795-4274
www.Xlibris.com
Orders@Xlibris.com

Print information available on the last page

Rev. date: 04/20/2016

Words of Praise for Wilhelmina Grant's A Feeling of Fullness: Insights of a Divinely Guided Journey Beyond Breast Cancer

Wilhelmina Grant, founder of SISTAAH (Survivors Inspiring Sisters Through Art & Advocacy for Health), has written a powerful book that is far more than another memoir about surviving breast cancer. It is a book about courage and believing in oneself completely. It is about following one's intuition in the face of professionally informed opinions. It is about having faith in spiritual guidance. In short, Ms. Grant has written a book for our times: a book about taking charge of one's destiny through combining what one had to do with what one loves to do. Ms. Grant found her calling by turning to art for healing and renewal.

Her first sentence "Cancer was the best thing that ever happened to me" may send shockwaves through the reader's mind, but it is a perfect introduction to Ms. Grant herself. Not simply a survivor, Ms. Grant is a "thriver," aiming for "a feeling of fullness" as she affirms being alive and healthy. Her extraordinary strength and resourcefulness helped her arrive at this desirable destination. Her book shares the journey to this realization, giving the reader a sense of how she made her decisions along the way.

However, to reach this goal, we discover a roller-coaster ride of outrageous fortune. From inexplicable breast pain that is, at first, trivialized by doctors, to unemployment after 9/11 to returning to college to discovering her artistic gifts. Ms. Grant may credit cancer as the "best thing that ever happened" to her, but in fact she teaches us how to turn "lemons into lemonade," as she writes: "I have discovered that the transformation of outdated, rusty and broken objects is a metaphor for personal growth, renewal and boundless possibilities. If life as a cancer survivor has given me lemons, then wellness advocacy through art-making has truly become my 'lemonade'." (*When Life Gives You Lemons*, 2010).

In response to great adversity, Wilhelmina Grant founded a sisterhood, SISTAAH, to educate women about breast cancer and early detection. As we read about Ms. Grant's journey to this place, we root for her all the way, because we have fallen in love with the protagonist of this thrilling story. We love her spunk and her drive, which comes through not only in her actions, but also in her words, her honesty and her natural verve. Thank goodness her energy found its way to making art, which is excellent. We find examples reproduced in photographs throughout these beautiful pages. Her visual work brings us even closer to understanding her indomitable spirit.

Therefore, Ms. Grant shares with us more than her struggle to survive cancer. She inspires us to find our true path in life, even in the face of enormous obstacles. And she demonstrates how to surmount these obstacles with sound choices, discipline and relentless resolve. In a world that seems fraught with so many possible directions at our disposal, this book is particularly relevant to those who feel the next chapter remains ahead, even if a mental GPS does not map out the precise course in advance. *A Feeling of Fullness: Insights of a Divinely Guided Journey Beyond Breast Cancer* encourages us to greet life's challenges with positivity and unexpected detours into serendipitous opportunities. Hopefully, Ms. Grant's book will reach a very wide audience that will benefit from her experienced advice and example.

Beth S. Gersh-Nesic, Ph.D.
Director, New York Arts Exchange (www.nyarts-exchange.com)

As the saying goes, "When life gives you lemons, make lemonade." Wilhelmina Grant's book, *A Feeling of Fullness: Insights of a Divinely Guided Journey Beyond Breast Cancer,* is an engaging, informative, inspirational cool drink of some of the best lemonade around.

Shouting survival by any means necessary, this is an honest and thorough account of conquering the fear, pain, and uncertainty of fighting and living a full life beyond breast cancer. Her personal journey, accompanied by photos of her engaging artwork, leads us through this warrior's fight to live, as it inspires us all to follow her lead. Like letters from an old friend you've been longing to hear from, she welcomes us to experience her journey, stating, "I recognize that everything that I have ever done has prepared me for everything that I will ever do, and that absolutely nothing has transpired by accident." Indeed, as cancer is that taboo word no one wants to hear, particularly in the African-American community where breast cancer deaths remain higher, Wilhelmina warns that not acknowledging it does not make it go away. While this is about her journey, it is also, and more importantly, an informative road guide for improving your own personal health, and living fully, knowing you have done all you could to remain healthy.

I first met this tall, stately, beautiful warrior at an October breast cancer awareness event shortly after she started SISTAAH. In this huge auditorium in Harlem, I was looking for women with stories to tell about their breast cancer journeys. Wilhelmina sat surrounded by her determination and her art. She was immediately engaging, explaining the array of collages of paper and objects, drawing me in with a specific purpose. I remember her proclaiming that as a breast cancer survivor, her art is activism. Indeed, you will marvel at her artwork displayed in this book, many made of discarded everyday objects, testimonies in themselves. She repurposes the once-useless trash from someone's past, making it anew. She writes, "I discovered that I could express anything that needed to be said using art." An amazing piece in this book is a perfect testament to the power of her art. *Many Woman* is a woman created from kitchen objects: a vegetable grater for her body, forks giving her legs, and the wooden handles of steel knives forming her open arms. But it is the blades of these knives defining her upper body that moved me most. On top of the steel blades rest two perfect looking breasts. Her face displays a huge smile. She lives — and that's the point! *A Feeling of Fullness: Insights of a Divinely Guided Journey Beyond Breast Cancer* will leave you filled with empowerment!

Bridgette A. Wimberly
Playwright, poet, librettist
Founding Director, *From Breast Cancer to Broadway*

Wilhelmina Grant has provided women everywhere with a true story of creativity and courage — and in the "cancer world," those words are rarely combined. Finding her own inner strength, coupled with a remarkable curiosity about EVERYTHING, including all the flotsam and jetsam of life, Wilhelmina has not only created an artistic world for herself, but has opened her heart and hands to anyone who will take the risk to create. Many have followed in her footsteps and have become artists themselves under her guidance — all the while coming to terms with the scariest three words in the English language: "You have cancer." It is Wilhelmina's strong belief in the power of creativity to heal the spirit that will resonate with others in similar challenging situations.

This book can be called a memoir, but a more apt description would be "a call to action" to all the women who should read it and seize the day — or the paintbrush, glue and scissors! Wilhelmina Grant is a rock star in both the cancer support community AND the art world!

Robin Glazer, Cancer Survivor
Executive Director, The Creative Center

For M., whose love, wisdom and strength are as enormous as the sea.

Churning Sea

DEDICATION

In commemoration of the stellar journeys of 13 prominent, trailblazing African-American women who lost their lives to breast cancer: May the memory of their strength, originality, leadership and courage continue to influence us as we strive to improve the health and longevity of our grandmothers, mothers, aunts, sisters, wives, cousins, nieces, daughters, partners, caregivers, mentors, friends and ourselves.

Time Into Eternity

Although there are countless others, I chose to highlight for this dedication the following 13 historic, ancestral African-American women who have impacted society significantly, and who would have undoubtedly made even greater accomplishments and contributions if they had lived longer, healthier lives. I pay homage to the following influential, intelligent and beautiful ancestors and acknowledge them by celebrating their humanity through a traveling memorial art exhibition (*Clock Strikes Thirteen*, 2010).

Fannie Lou Hamer (1917-1977) was instrumental in organizing the Student Nonviolent Coordinating Committee (SNCC), and later became the Vice-Chair of the Mississippi Freedom Democratic Party. *"I'm Sick and Tired of Being Sick and Tired"* — Fannie Lou Hamer's gravestone epitaph.

June Jordan (1936-2002) Poet, novelist, essayist, activist, professor of English at City College, Sarah Lawrence College, Yale University, and Connecticut College. She was awarded a Rockefeller Grant and Congressional recognition for her work in the progressive and civil rights movements. She was mentored by Fannie Lou Hamer.

Hattie McDaniel (1895-1952) Singer, songwriter, comedienne, stage actress, radio performer. She was the first African-American woman to sing on radio in America; has TWO stars on the Hollywood Walk of Fame; and was the first African-American Academy Award winner.

Audre Lorde (1934-1992) Writer, poet, essayist, educator, mother, feminist, lesbian, warrior. In 1980, she published the autobiographical *The Cancer Journals,* courageously writing about her mastectomy and her decision to pursue alternate treatment when the cancer recurred.

Minnie Riperton (1947-1979) Singer, songwriter, noted for a vocal range of five octaves. Diagnosed in 1976, Minnie was one of the first celebrities to publicly announce her breast cancer diagnosis and become a cancer activist.

Naomi Sims (1948-2009) Model, author, businesswoman. A photograph of Naomi was featured on the cover of *Ladies Home Journal;* she was the first African-American woman to be displayed prominently on a national magazine. She created a successful wig collection, then eventually expanded her businesses into a multimillion-dollar beauty empire.

Danitra Vance (1954-1994) Actress, playwright, first African-American woman to be part of the Repertory Players on *Saturday Night Live*. After her surgery she wrote and performed a skit entitled "The Radical Girl's Guide to Radical Mastectomy." She was given an *NAACP* Image Award in 1986 and later won an Obie for her performance in the theatrical adaptation of *Spunk*, a collection of short stories by Zora Neale Hurston.

Rosalind Cash (1938-1995) Singer and stage, screen and television actress; an original member of The Negro Ensemble Company. She was nominated for an Emmy for *Go Tell It on the Mountain,* and an NAACP Image Award for *Sister, Sister.*

Syreeta Wright (1946-2004) Singer, songwriter, composer. In addition to her own numerous compositions, she collaborated with former husband Stevie Wonder on many musical creations including "Signed, Sealed Delivered," "If You Really Love Me," and "It's a Shame."

Roxie Roker (1929-1995) Stage and screen actress best known for her groundbreaking role in an interracial marriage on the primetime show *The Jeffersons*. She won an Obie and was nominated for a Tony. She received a citation for her humanitarian efforts as a children's advocate in Los Angeles.

Shirley Horn (1934-2005) Jazz pianist and vocalist who revived her career in her 50s, she won a *Grammy* and was recognized by the National Endowment for the Arts as a Jazz Master for lifelong contributions to jazz.

Patricia Roberts Harris (1924-1985) First African-American woman appointed to a presidential cabinet (Carter) as Secretary of Housing and Urban Development (HUD). She also was the former executive director of Delta Sigma Theta Sorority and the International Ambassador to Luxembourg.

Alaina Reed-Amini (1946-2009) Singer and actress on Broadway and Off-Broadway, film and television. She appeared in *Sgt. Pepper's Lonely Hearts Club Band, Hair, Chicago* and *Eubie.* Memorable television roles include Olivia on *Sesame Street* and Rose on *227.*

Contents

FOREWORD

I know Wilhelmina Grant as a friend, fighter, foremost as a survivor. She is not just a two-time breast cancer survivor, she is a survivor of life. Over the last two decades she has embraced the challenges that have come her way with grace, dignity and tenacity. Her free spirit has allowed her to soar above the storm as she has sailed into a place of perpetual peace.

Being diagnosed with breast cancer in her late thirties made her understand that breast cancer doesn't discriminate when it comes to age. As she jumped over hurdles to navigate through her own personal health crises, she became an advocate for other African-American women and those who are medically underserved so that they could benefit from early detection.

In order to help other women understand how your pain can press you into your purpose, Wilhelmina has become transparent through the pages of her book *A Feeling of Fullness: Insights of a Divinely Guided Journey Beyond Breast Cancer*. Within the next few pages you will realize that her testimony has been sculptured by the divine fingertips of God.

Lie back and relax as you read her amazing story. There is no doubt that as you read the steps that Wilhelmina has taken in her journey toward health, you realize that you will win if you don't quit. Let her words inspire you as you embark on your own personal journey to wellness.

Sylvia Dunnavant
Award-winning Author and Motivational Speaker
Founder of the *Celebrating Life Foundation*

PREFACE

Cancer is probably the best thing that ever happened to me! That may be a strange and unlikely statement to make, but I believe that instead of taking things away from me, the cancer experience has changed my life in innumerable ways. Some of the things that I have done, the people that I have met and the places that I have been would never have been possible if it were not for the diagnosis of cancer. After overcoming cancer twice, I feel like I am abundantly blessed. However, on both of those occasions, seven years apart, when I heard the words "you have cancer," my diagnosis had almost been overlooked, ignored or disregarded. After I endured surgery, heavy-dose chemotherapy, radiation, and hormone therapy, I am now cancer-free, and celebrating 22 years of survivorship and counting… And I am living a life beyond my wildest dreams, full of energy, creativity, peace of mind, love and joy.

However, sadly, over the years, I have been a witness to dozens of lives taken by breast cancer. Unfortunately, scores of my peers and others in the community came to their diagnoses late, and others who were aware of their disease, refused appropriate treatment because of fear or barriers to access of care. I personally have no aversion to holistic treatments, herbal preparations and "natural" remedies. Indeed, I included various non-traditional approaches to augment the medical treatment, and coordinated with my medical team to be sure that I did not compromise my treatment or damage my health during the process. But most of all, I attribute my healing and longevity to my faith and belief in the omnipotent power of God.

This book chronicles the journey from the nearly-missed diagnosis of Stage II-A breast cancer at age 37, through my present-day life as an artist/health awareness advocate. I felt that it would be selfish of me to silently sit by and watch the continual devastation without lifting my hands and voice to share my experiences in hopes of helping others. My determination to interact with community members and encourage them to be proactive about their healthcare began shortly after my diagnosis in 1994. Accordingly, I became a community outreach coordinator for a local breast cancer support services organization. It was indeed healing and empowering to lift my voice throughout my recovery process. It is equally important that I continue breaking the silence today.

ACKNOWLEDGEMENTS

"It takes a village to raise a child." — Nigerian proverb

I am grateful for the "village" where I spent my formative years as a child.

Baby Wilhelmina seated on ground front row, center, with extended family in Clarendon County, South Carolina, ca. 1958

ACKNOWLEDGEMENTS

In honor of the Creator, Ancestors, Spirit Guides and Orisas for all of their blessings;

In memory of my parents: Daisy F. Bennett and William E. Grant for passing along their gifts of fortitude, resilience, creativity, and sense of humor; in memory of my grandparents: William H. Grant, Fannie Athalia Grant, David Jenkins and Hester Wilhelmina Jenkins for their loving care and old-fashioned upbringing; in memory of my first cancer mentor and mentee, Estelle Hill and Oni Faida Lampley;

To my Godparents/Elders: John Robinson, Carole Robinson, Linda Evans, Ted Brooks, Craig Brown, and Alberto Oceguera for spiritual guidance, direction and training;

To Yvette C. Grant, the protective, quintessential big sister, and all of my loving siblings and extended family; to D.G. Wilson-Davis, confidante and mentor; Freda Macon, my longest, steadfast friend; Sylvia Dunnavant, comrade and an amazing writer, photographer, and powerful example of belief in miracles;

Thank you, Miriam Levy, M.D., for taking the preemptive action leading to the early diagnosis, which undeniably contributed to the extension of my life; to Dr. Alison Estabrook, surgeon, Dr. Gregory Mears, oncologist, and the cadre of nurses: I appreciate your excellence;

To the Center for Anti-Violence Education/Brooklyn Women's Martial Arts for helping me learn how to build strength, discipline, and fearlessness, and how to develop an increased sense of empowerment and unapologetic assuredness of my right to occupy space in the world; to Dee Lent, fellow karate practitioner who unknowingly delivered the life-saving lucky punch; and to Mary Alford, Geleni Fontaine and Yvette Robinson for being my armor bearers throughout the rough times during early diagnosis and treatment;

To SHARE For Women With Breast or Ovarian Cancer for empowering women and families for decades; to The Creative Center at University Settlement for the use of the arts in healthcare to enable cancer survivors to uncover personal expression and creativity;

Appreciation to Susan G. Komen® for permission to reprint *Facts for Life – Breast Cancer Resources*;

Thank you Mary McQueen Alford, M.A., and Godfrey Gregg, Ph.D., for your expertise, patience and assistance in editing this book. Gratitude to Beth S. Gersh-Nesic, Ph.D., Robin Glazer and Bridgette A. Wimberly for their gracious reviews.

INTRODUCTION

Chilling in the Engine

A Feeling of Fullness: Insights of a Divinely Guided Journey Beyond Breast Cancer is a testimonial about my transformation after diagnosis and the triumph of making an impact in the community. I know that I have been continually and divinely guided on my life's journey throughout the passage of time. I recognize that everything that I have ever done has prepared me for everything that I will ever do; and that absolutely nothing has transpired by accident.

My former occupation as a flight attendant allowed me to travel both nationally and internationally to venues where I shared my experiences with likeminded warriors. My training and involvement as a Gynecological Teaching Associate in medical schools throughout New York State primed me with expertise on breast examination techniques that I shared as a lay health educator. My martial arts training has helped me to develop focus, discipline, determination and a fearless fighting spirit. I gather the sum of those experiences to further my breast health initiatives that benefit communities.

We know that art is a universal language of symbols and images that succeeds in speaking to the heart, mind and spirit in a way that transcends verbal expression. Accordingly, at age 52, when I discovered my artistic ability, I began using art as an informational and inspirational tool to further my health awareness mission. In my art-making, I gather and repurpose discarded everyday objects by creatively arranging them. The resulting compositions illustrate the importance of early detection of breast cancer, and survivorship —

subjects which remain a taboo discussion for too many, especially in the African-American community. Moreover, during the viewing of my art, participants are more apt to initiate discussion about the significance of what they have seen and learned during the exhibition. I do not purport to have answers to the sociological and epidemiological questions about the reasons for health disparities. However, I am delighted that after viewing the art, the way is open to dialogue amongst people who would not previously utter the word "cancer."

Solo Kata

When Life Gives You
Lemons

As a non-drawing artist, I work through an alternative means of artistic expression in visual arts – assemblage, which is like painting with objects. Making assemblages using found objects and discarded items, whether the items are acquired at a thrift shop, found on a curbside or received from friends who collect things on my behalf, represents a re-evaluation of the life cycle of everyday items in our throwaway society. I have discovered that the transformation of outdated, rusty, or broken objects is a metaphor for personal growth, renewal and boundless possibilities. If life as a cancer survivor has given me lemons, then wellness advocacy through art-making has truly become my "lemonade."

DISSED AND DISMISSED

I was 37 years old and quite the vision of health and fitness. It was the spring of 1994 and I had been practicing karate a few times a week. One day I was in a sparring match, a pretend fight with a fellow student, when I took a really hard punch to the left side of my chest. I kept fighting because I did not want to lose the contest, but I was in a lot of pain. After three weeks had passed I was still feeling sharp and shooting pains in my left breast. As a practitioner of karate, however, I knew this pain was beyond the ordinary. This was pain which I had never experienced.

So while juggling my busy schedule as a full-time international flight attendant, a part-time college student, and an intern at a downtown museum, I took myself, full of optimism and medical insurance, to a breast clinic and asked for a mammogram. My request was refused because I did not have a doctor's referral and because I was under age 40. Instead, the medical provider performed an ultrasound and informed me that the constant pain and palpable lump in my breast was a complex cyst. He said I could either make an appointment to have the cyst drained

High Kick

or better yet, just leave it alone. And for the pain, he suggested that I could apply warm or cold compresses. I will never forget that doctor's words nor his demeanor. As he patted the back of my hand, he told me:

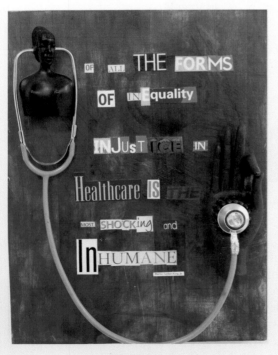
Injustice and Inequality

"Don't worry, my dear; it is not cancer." "At age 37," he said, "you are much too young to have breast cancer. Besides, cancer does not run in your family and it does not strike Black women that often. Most of all, if a lump is painful, it is not cancer. You really don't have anything to be concerned about."

Clearly, he made that determination without the evidence of an investigative mammogram or a biopsy. I was angry, upset and in severe pain, and left his office in tears. I went to my gynecologist's office to request a mammography referral. Unfortunately, he concurred with the opinion of the clinic — that I did not need a mammogram. I immediately fired him and appealed to his associate, who forthwith provided me with a mammography referral and appointment.

THE DIAGNOSIS

Discombobulated

I went to a radiology center where they listened to me and did a thorough investigation which included a mammogram, ultrasound, clinical breast exam, and needle biopsy. Back in 1994, diagnostic breast biopsies were typically done in the operating room, but fortunately, I was examined by a concerned and talented radiologist/physician who performed the needle biopsy in her office that same day. As it turned out, that blow to the breast during karate practice revealed a growth the size of a pearl which was hiding on the back portion of the breast on my chest wall. The tumor was in an area that was inaccessible and would likely be missed on a mammogram. If it had not been for that lucky punch which caused the extreme pain, the tumor may have gone unnoticed until it was too late. If it were not for the bold, knowledgeable, and confident radiologist, my story would be quite different. The post-surgical pathology report after surgery revealed a diagnosis of Stage II-A Infiltrating Ductal Carcinoma with Positive Lymph Node Involvement.

Besides almost falling through the cracks of the medical system, my mental and emotional well-being was constantly being challenged. I had to endure a barrage of thoughtless and appalling things that people said to me when I confided in them about my diagnosis and upcoming breast surgery. Folks said things like:

"I can't imagine not having you around."

"Oh, now you can get a free boob job."

"You should take some shark cartilage."

"Now at least you know what you're going to die from!"

One associate even sent a greeting card to me in the mail that said "With Sympathy."

I was literally getting sick from all of the unsolicited, ignorant and annoying comments and advice. I stopped communicating with people and appointed one close friend, Yvette to be my spokesperson. My stock response was:

"I cannot have this discussion with you right now. Please go talk to Yvette. She can tell you everything you need to know."

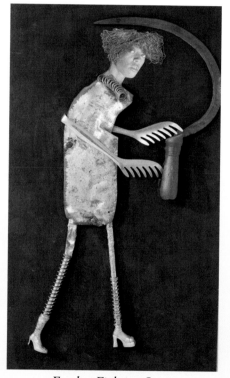

Fearless Fighting Spirit

Thank goodness I had my support group members to help calm my fears and my strong armor bearers to deflect the ignorance of the well-intended.

After a series of surgical consultations which included a second and third opinion, I decided upon a procedure: lumpectomy, surgical removal of the lump, along with an axillary node dissection to verify the extent of lymph node involvement. The tumor was positioned at the bottom of the breast and the lump could be removed easily without disfiguring the breast. After the surgery, I would undergo chemotherapy and radiation to eradicate any remaining cancer cells. I had never undergone surgery or anesthesia before and I was extremely nervous. On the morning of the surgery, as they made preparations to administer the anesthesia, I was shaking so much that the nurse covered me a warm blanket. But I was not shivering from the cold, I was shaking from fright. At that very moment, I decided that if I came through the surgery, that

I would fight like mad to overcome anything else that might lie ahead. I recited Psalm 23 as they wheeled me into the operating room. The next thing I heard was "Miss Grant, open your eyes and take a deep breath." The surgery was over, I was in the recovery room, and the next phase of my journey had begun.

THE TREATMENT

After extensive research, I chose an aggressive course of chemotherapy using Adriamycin, Taxol and Cytoxan, three cycles of each in three large doses, administered one week on and one week off. I did not have a normal regimen. I had a more intensive course of treatment. The final three treatments to administer Cytoxan required hospitalization for three days each time for extra pre- and post-infusion hydration and observation. Additionally, for the entire duration of the chemotherapy I was required to self-inject a bone marrow stimulating drug for ten consecutive days after each treatment to help restore the red and white blood cell count. The injections were was necessary in order for me to tolerate the bombardment of drugs. Side effects of the chemo were very drastic, and uncomfortable, albeit brief and temporary. I had my first round of Adriamycin on July 5, 1994. The initial dose of chemo halted my menstrual cycle, causing chemically-induced menopause. The vein in my arm where the chemo was administered became darkened

Kicking Cancer to the Curb

and hard. I endured, at different intervals, severe bone pain, muscle pain and joint pain, as each medication came with its own set of reactions. My nails and the inside of my mouth (including my tongue) became discolored a bluish black, and of course my hair fell out. Other than the visible side effects the outside world was unaware of my experiences. I joined a group for women recently diagnosed with breast cancer. We shared notes and experiences. We helped each other cope. We talked about feelings and discussed issues too emotionally difficult to discuss with loved ones.

Bald and Beautiful

It was suggested by the group's facilitator that I get a wig early on. I had already purchased a $200 human hair wig and had it cut and styled to look more natural. After that, I went to a barber and had my hair, which I had grown into beautifully formed dreadlocks, cropped very short to make the anticipated hair loss seem less dramatic. I was not ready to part with my beloved hair, so I took the clipped locks home in a paper bag. Suddenly on July 14 while I was shampooing, my hair follicles seemed to release my hair all at once. Hair stuck to everything: the shower curtain, my skin, the tub — reminding me of a scene from a scary movie. The baldness lasted four months.

Ocean Frolic

By then I had become accustomed to drawing on eyebrows and enjoying the feeling of baby soft, hairless skin. I never did wear that $200 wig. Many months later after treatment was finished, I went on vacation in Mexico. I took the bag of clipped hair to the ocean, dropped it in and let it go! I was ready for a new beginning.

SURVIVOR

I am exceedingly grateful for having been part of the compassionate martial arts center where I trained. Not only did the discipline of martial arts help me to focus on my healing, but the dojo's philosophy was one of helping vulnerable people become empowered. Instead of feeling sorry for myself, I put my energy into telling my story and encouraging everyone who would listen about the value of early detection and advocating for themselves.

Survivor

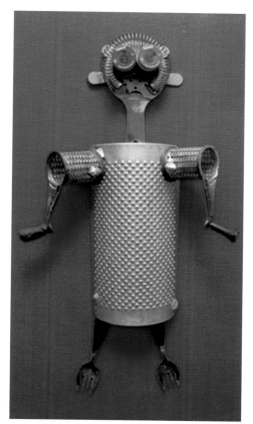

Eagle Eyed Grateful Lady

As time went on I continued learning new things and becoming more involved in breast cancer awareness activism. Because I was appalled that I had been dissed and dismissed by the medical establishment, I was spurred into action knowing that there was very little information, accommodation, and accessibility available in my community. I was sure that the same thing that happened to me could happen to someone else. The first doctor that I encountered was correct in stating that Black women are not diagnosed with breast cancer as often as white women, but he did not mention the statistic that Black women tend to die almost twice as often. My first mentor and support group facilitator saw some potential in my outreach efforts and encouraged me to get more deeply involved in the community. In a speech that she wrote shortly before she passed away, Estelle Hill declared "There is much more work to be done."

Shortly afterward, my breast cancer awareness crusade increased. I continued to share the cancer awareness and survivorship message throughout the mid-1990s, a time when people were just beginning to become more comfortable about saying and hearing the word "cancer" and not the often repeated euphemism "the Big C."

I knew that there was immense stigma, fear, secrecy, silent suffering and misinformation running rampant within the Black community. But something else that I learned was that women and men held many erroneous beliefs and negative attitudes about breast cancer. I heard statements such as:

"No wife of mine is going to walk around with one breast."

"I wouldn't marry half a woman."

"Once they cut you open, the cancer will spread everywhere."

"I'm afraid that my man will leave me…"

"I was born with these breasts and I'm gonna die with these breasts." (Yes. You just might.)

Less Diagnosis But More Death

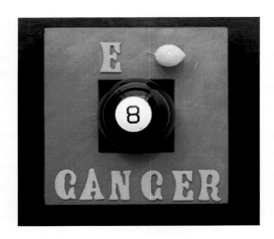

*Eliminate Cancer
(African-Americans
Behind the 8-Ball)*

Many people also expressed beliefs such as the popular assumption that breast cancer automatically means surgical removal of the breast. One of the main messages that I would be sure to deliver is that if the cancer is detected early enough, the surgical procedures can be minimal. Furthermore, reconstruction to restore the appearance of the breast after surgery is an option if a woman so chooses. Some people seem to presume a fatalistic outcome when it comes to cancer. What they do not realize is that cancer is just a word, not a sentence — particularly not a death sentence if cancer is detected early.

ALMOST SLIPPING THROUGH THE CRACKS

Fast-forwarding to seven years later… In 2001 my health was normal, things in my life were going great, but my periodic mammograms were looking a little suspicious and warranted further investigation. After the experience in 1994, my medical team had been kept on speed-dial! If anything appeared abnormal I wanted to know immediately. The occasion arose for a biopsy to investigate suspicious micro-calcifications. I underwent a core biopsy procedure and awaited the results.

A week went by and there was no news. Another week passed, and again no news. As the saying goes, "No news is good news," right? Wrong! As it turned out, I had not been notified of the biopsy results and my medical file had been returned to the shelf. Someone in the office thought someone else had notified me, meanwhile, no one notified me; I had to be persistent and vigilant in obtaining the biopsy results. Following repeated calls I finally got the news. The pathology report showed DCIS (Ductal Carcinoma in Situ) Stage Zero. I was diagnosed with breast cancer again, but this time, it was non-invasive. Thankfully, no chemotherapy or radiation was required. According to the surgeon, the new diagnosis would not have any effect on my life expectancy. The only medical treatment after surgery would be a regimen of aromatase inhibitors.

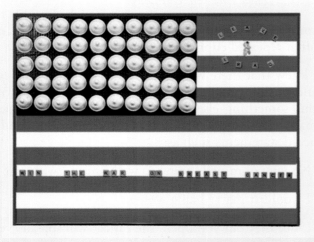

Breasts, Bandages and Red Tape

Girl Talk

To keep things as simple as possible, I decided upon mastectomy without reconstruction as a surgical procedure. However, I was a little surprised that the insurance would pay for a hospital room for only one day. The surgeon scheduled my surgery accordingly, so that I would be released 23 hours after I was admitted. I experienced what they call a "drive-through mastectomy." The surgery went well and I spent Thursday night in the hospital knowing full well that I would have to be out by a certain hour on Friday morning. During my brief hospital stay I found it comical that everybody who came to check on me on an hourly basis asked to see my dressing. I complied each time by opening my gown and showing my bandages to each surgeon, nurse, physical therapist, and more nurses. The bandages were extremely tight, clean and dry. There was no seepage of blood or evidence of anything unusual. Early on Friday morning, I was released to go home to rest and recover.

On Saturday afternoon, to my intense horror, the area where the left breast used to be was grossly swollen, discolored, and resembled a jumbo eggplant attached to my chest. I called the doctor's answering service in a state of panic. I first spoke to the physician's assistant, who took notes based on information that I gave her. I then spoke to the physician-on-call, who recommended that I return to the hospital for emergency surgery. It seems as though my body does not play by any of the cancer rules! I had developed a hematoma, which typically occurs within the first 24 hours after surgery, thus the constant monitoring of my dressing while I was in the hospital bed. The hematoma appeared 48 hours after surgery. However, I chose to wait until after the weekend, when my personal surgeon rather than the ER surgeon could reopen the wound, release the excess coagulated blood, and reapply the stitches. I traveled back to the hospital on Monday; the surgeon removed the hematoma under local anesthesia, installed a drainage tube in my side, and allowed me to return home.

A FORK IN THE ROAD ON THE CANCER JOURNEY

**Borough of Manhattan
Community College
Commencement 2004**   ISLAND PHOTOGRAPHY

Community College 2004

After the second cancer diagnosis in early 2001 I breezed through the healing process. The site of the surgery and hematoma healed and I was as good as new in a matter of weeks. However, I needed time away from working in the cancer community because I felt as though I could no longer be an effective spokesperson for breast cancer awareness. I needed to get my confidence back after being re-diagnosed. I continued working as a flight attendant for a while, but the job unexpectedly vanished after the events of September 11, since the airline that I worked for was directly affected. During the airline layoff, I was still not ready to resume health advocacy work, so I became an executive assistant.

I decided to return to college after a long hiatus following my first diagnosis. I enrolled in community college and registered for the 17 credits that I needed to complete my Associate's Degree. I graduated with honors and transferred to a four year college.

I was able to qualify for a scholarship because my airline job was eliminated as a result of the terrorist attacks on September 11. Luckily, my tuition and fees were further subsidized by grants and scholarships during the following two years of college. Serendipitously, one afternoon while I was shopping on 125th Street in Harlem for curtains for the office, I was compelled to walk into one of the big-box stores that had recently opened. I had never been inside the store, and although they sold housewares, I did not think that they sold curtains. Still, I felt the urge to go inside. Lo and behold, the first person I saw as I stepped off the escalator was a former airline colleague, who informed me that, as a laid-off airline employee, I was eligible for a grant to obtain occupational retraining for another career, or funding to go to college. Shortly afterward, I went to the company's headquarters in St. Louis, filled out the necessary paperwork and received an educational grant for $10,000, which covered my tuition and books for the remainder of my undergraduate studies.

As my graduation date approached, I applied to the college for a scholarship to graduate school, intending to study Cultural Anthropology. As I became busy dealing with everyday responsibilities, I had totally forgotten about the scholarship application. On graduation day, as I proudly marched into the massive auditorium at Radio City Music Hall, my eyes welled up with tears. I was elated that I would finally receive my Bachelor's Degree after delays adding up to 32 years post-high school.

Bachelor of Arts 2006

My excitement turned to disappointment when I searched the program booklet and failed to find my name listed along with my classmates who were also receiving degrees from the English Department. I was slated for September completion because I was missing two credits which I would earn over the summer. For that reason, I was not entitled to have my name printed on the Commencement Program, even though I was allowed to march with my fellow classmates. Eventually, my disappointment turned to gratitude and joy when my name was announced as a recipient of a generous scholarship to graduate school. When I arrived home that afternoon I found the congratulatory letter in my mailbox! I began graduate studies that fall in the Urban Affairs and Planning Department at Hunter College and continued working at a small non-profit cultural organization in Harlem.

The year 2008 turned out to be an extremely harrowing time for me. My employment at the non-profit organization was unexpectedly terminated during that winter. I was also mentally and emotionally distraught, as I was still mourning my mother's death from lung cancer and my cousin's murder. To make things worse, I suddenly became single and had no companion's shoulder to lean on while going through challenges; these challenges continued to mount throughout the subsequent months. It was the penultimate semester before earning my Master's degree, the scholarship money was depleted, and I had very little cash and savings. My employment at the non-profit did not include health insurance, therefore, and I had been paying those fees out-of-pocket. I had to choose between paying for tuition and books, or paying for health insurance. Shortly after allowing my health insurance to lapse, I developed lymphedema — a circulatory disorder that stemmed from the axillary node dissection 14 years earlier, in which 25 lymph nodes were removed from my left armpit in order to stage the breast cancer diagnosis. Lymphedema is an irreversible but manageable swelling that can appear at any time, even many years after surgery. Surprisingly, there are very few medical professionals who truly understand the complexities and proper treatment of lymphedema, and the waiting list for treatment is lengthy.

During that time I was at my wit's end and doing all to persevere despite the physical pain and disfigurement of my left arm. Because I no longer had an income or insurance, I qualified for Medicaid to get treatment for the lymphedema. However, it took many months and much persistence to receive the proper physical therapy.

Grace Under Pressure

TRASH INTO TREASURE

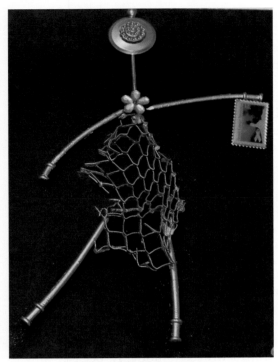

Stamp Out Breast Cancer

The saving grace was that art entered my life in a significant and unexpected way at age 52. This is how it happened. To keep myself busy, and to keep from being depressed I decided to enjoy doing artistic projects. I viewed some assemblage artworks that were created by a neighborhood artist, who encouraged me to try putting found objects together. He suggested some types of adhesives and substrates to use. I soon discovered that I had a flair for making found-object assemblage art. This was a pivotal moment in my life. I developed the idea of combining my artistry with a social message. The result was a breast cancer awareness art collection; some of the works are highlighted in this book. I had become an emerging artist.

It was incredibly gratifying to create the *Hot Comb Series*. Each hot comb artwork gave birth to the next, as I kept receiving gifts of hot combs from women who no longer use them. The hot comb is a relic that many women in the African-American community identify with. I created and photographed the artworks, printed up art cards and distributed them at neighborhood hair salons. The art cards included a caption: *"If you can sit in a beauty parlor for hours on a regular basis awaiting your turn to tolerate the hot comb, then you can show up for an annual mammogram! Early detection saves lives."*

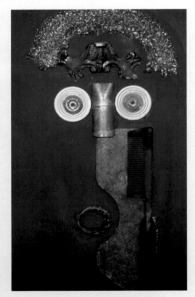

Tolerating the Hot Comb

Tolerating the Hot Comb-2

Hot Comb in the Kitchen

Hot Comb in the Kitchen-2

Dyed, Fried and Laid to the Side

I discovered that I could express anything by using art. I remember an artwork that I created entitled *Maternal Mortality* which was initially meant to respond to a call for art for an exhibition. The exhibition dealt with worldwide deaths of women during childbirth due to preventable complications. Subsequent to that exhibition, that piece has revealed additional, deeper meaning reflecting my personal experience. As a 37-year-old breast cancer patient who underwent chemotherapy in 1994, I was informed of the probable loss of fertility, but I was not offered information concerning egg conservation for possible future pregnancy. In the mid-1990s, the egg-preserving procedure was not as common as it is today, but it was being implemented, as I found out from other patients of child-bearing age, who were privileged to safeguard their eggs and achieve post-cancer pregnancies.

Maternal Mortality/Shambled Eggs

After my mastectomy, I became very disturbed by the suggestion that I should consider breast implants or employ some other remedy to look more womanly. I was very annoyed at the notion that I might be considered incomplete. I wrote the following essay *Say It Loud, I'm Flat and Proud!* to express an alternative point of view. I also created an artwork bearing the same title.

Contrary to popular belief, not all women are willing to make certain sacrifices to conform to today's societal dictates of fashion and sexual attractiveness. I personally do not buy into the ideal of a particular physical standard constituting beauty and self-worth. As a survivor of breast cancer (twice) I chose to forego all of the post-mastectomy options mentioned below which would have enabled me to comply with the world's expectation of how my body should look. Years ago, as I investigated the post-mastectomy breast appearance issue, I discovered that reconstruction *is* a practical option for some women.

First, there is the TRAM flap reconstruction, using tissue from the belly area, which transforms belly fat into a breast mound. But a plastic surgeon would be hard pressed to locate enough tissue from my sparsely endowed abdomen to fashion a mound even remotely resembling a mammary gland. That was an option that I abandoned very quickly. Then I considered the purchase of a simple synthetic, padded undergarment, but found it hot and constricting. As well, neither the once-popular gel-filled, or water-filled cups, nor the air-filled pump-up bras would do me justice.

The traditional, albeit expensive, prosthesis preferred by some women does not exist in size double-A (why would it)? The "A"-cup looked and felt disproportionately large, heavy and unnatural to me. Another alternative, surgical implants, was a possibility, but that choice would initiate a perpetual relationship with the plastic surgeon. And, in my case, I would have needed bilateral implants even though I had surgery on only one breast. I was advised that a silicone implant — translation: poison — would be used to replace the removed breast, and a saline implant would be inserted under the unaffected breast to make both breasts symmetrical in appearance. Beside the fact that implants are not a one shot deal, it might take a minimum of three surgeries to get the breast augmentation process completed. Also, implants must be replaced from time to time. And that depends on everything going well with the implants: that they are not recalled by the manufacturer for springing a leak, deflating, petrifying, becoming infected, or migrating to other areas of the body. The other aspect of surgical implants is the medical insurance issue. Although I did have medical insurance at the time of the mastectomy, shortly afterward, the airline downsized. I became unemployed and uninsured. Imagine my dilemma if I had been in the midst of a breast implantation process. Needless to say, my response to the implant option was an instant but polite "No, thank you!"

I maintain that for myself, declining all of the above was a sound decision. I am satisfied and comfortable to live in the strong, healthy, well-functioning, beautiful body that I possess. I am certain that at the end of my days, I would rather be remembered for the capacity of the heart within my chest rather than the appearance of the flesh atop it. I am proud and happy to be having a full and productive life which includes spiritual centeredness, a loving family, valued friendships, intimate companionship, an advanced college degree, an occupation of trust and responsibility, and the opportunity to pursue creative interests.

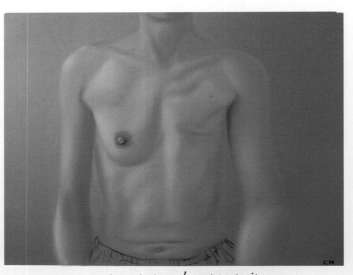

post-mastectomy breast portrait

In other words, after the mastectomy I chose to spend my time, energy and resources living a full life instead of filling my bra cups. And I can say with complete assurance that all of my progress, contentment and accomplishments are attributable to factors other than the appearance of a pair of perky, symmetrical breasts.

 In 2010 a fellow artist invited me to sit for a breast portrait and participate in a project which, at that time, tallied over 500 women of varying ages, body types, and physical characteristics. Some participants' bodies displayed scars and some did not. I am grateful for the experience and inclusion in the artist's exhibition catalogue, *Radical Acceptance*.

SISTAAH COMES TO LIFE

As I was working toward my Master's Degree in Urban Affairs at Hunter College in 2009, I developed an idea for an academic project which involved using the arts to engage the community and solve a problem regarding a public health issue — breast cancer awareness. My idea was rejected by my student colleagues, who opted instead to have our group project involve research and make recommendations which address the affordable housing crisis.

Consequently, after graduation I resurrected the idea and founded SISTAAH (Survivors Inspiring Sisters Through Art & Advocacy for Health, Inc.), whose mission is to inform, encourage and facilitate access to early detection of breast cancer by helping to connect the medically underserved to free screening services. SISTAAH seeks to enlighten the community and help change attitudes about cancer by presenting myself and other survivors as positive examples of cancer survivorship. SISTAAH's projects use the arts to communicate, increase the visibility of survivors, and emphasize the importance of early detection. Improvement of breast cancer survival rates is crucial for African-American women, a population that suffers a disproportionately higher rate of mortality despite being diagnosed less often than women in other ethnic groups.

Grad School 2009

SISTAAH is committed to sharing the breast health message, beginning with Harlem, the neighborhood where I reside, and subsequently extending the SISTAAH model to communities beyond Harlem. SISTAAH hopes that through greater health awareness education, and referrals for resources to provide screenings, detection of cancer in underserved communities possibly will occur at an early stage, increasing the potential for successful treatment and long-term survivorship.

Do The Right Thing, Get A Mammogram

Fan Giveaway in the Park

Using SISTAAH, Inc. as a platform, I launched two successful grant-funded community projects: *Saving Our Sisters in the African-American Community* and the *Harlem Hand Fan Initiative*. *Saving Our Sisters in the African-American Community* was a part of a health initiative sponsored by our local state senator, and engaged visual artists and cancer survivors in activism to promote early detection of breast cancer. Each artist/activist who participated in this art-based awareness-raising activity identified women in the community for whom substantial time had elapsed since their last mammogram, providing them with information for no-cost screening at The Breast Examination Center of Harlem (BECH), a partner with SISTAAH in this project.

In December 2010 the *Caring & Sharing Advent Service* sponsored by the A.M.E. Ministerial Alliance of New York took place at St. Luke A.M.E. Church in Harlem, New York. The SISTAAH crew delivered 2,500 art emblazoned hand fans bearing an informative health message.

The *SISTAAH Hand Fan Project*, funded by Susan G. Komen Greater New York Affiliate, seeks to spread awareness and encourage early detection of breast cancer. More than 200 clergy plus congregants attended. From the pulpit the pastor voiced his support for the *Hand Fan Project* and encouraged A.M.E. Ministerial Alliance members to take a supply of fans to their respective churches. SISTAAH volunteers distributed the contents of ten boxes to the A.M.E. Ministerial Alliance Members who would then disseminate them among 50 churches throughout New York State.

2,500 Fans

Another well-attended SISTAAH event, *A Night of Illumination*, a Women's History Month Art Exhibition and Community Event, was presented at Work Space Harlem Art Gallery. The Harlem Youth Marine Cadets Marching Band led a procession around the neighborhood followed by an energetic group of cancer survivors, artists, and community members chanting early-detection slogans and waving bright pink illuminated glowsticks. The lively procession and the color pink alerted the community to the disproportionately high rate of mortality in African-American women. For even greater impact, SISTAAH had contacted the Empire State Building Lighting Partner; the Empire State Building's colored lights, visible to the uptown marchers that evening, beamed bright pink to signify breast cancer awareness and activism.

In the course of creating SISTAAH programming, I was dismayed to discover that there were no survivorship celebrations held in Harlem during National Cancer Survivor's Month, so in 2010, I created one. Thus, the first annual Survivorship Sunday in Harlem, sponsored by our local state senator, celebrated the survivorship of cancer in women and men in the Harlem community. Survivorship Sunday in Harlem united cancer survivors, caregivers, family, friends and healthcare professionals to honor survivors for their strength and courage, and to recognize the contributions of their supporters. The event was attended by 150 guests and featured Hoda Kotb, co-anchor of *The Today Show* and *Dateline NBC*. Kotb, a breast cancer survivor, was keynote speaker for the event, and shared her story about her diagnosis, treatment and survivorship.

One of my favorite art shows, and the most poignant that I have created thus far, is *Clock Strikes Thirteen* (2010), a traveling exhibition which pays homage to 13 historic African-American women ancestors who have made a significant impact on society, and who undoubtedly would have enjoyed even greater accomplishments if they had lived longer, healthier lives. The women that are represented in the exhibition include: Fannie Lou Hamer, Hattie McDaniel, Audre Lorde, Minnie Riperton, Naomi Sims, Danitra Vance, June Jordan, Rosalind Cash, Syreeta Wright, Roxie Roker, Shirley Horn, Patricia Roberts Harris, and Alaina Reed-Amini. These women were trailblazers who made historic and momentous contributions. Sadly, only four of these heroines lived past age 60.

The *Clock Strikes Thirteen* exhibition also underscores the statistics that suggest that although incidence of diagnosis is about the same for white and African-American women, younger African-American women (under 45) have a higher incidence than white women.

Clock Strikes Thirteen also emphasizes the fact that one woman is diagnosed with breast cancer every three minutes, and one woman in the United States will die of breast cancer every 13 minutes. [Cancer Facts and Figures 2012, American Cancer Society]

CONCLUSION

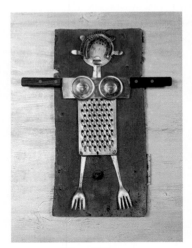

Many Woman

I am gladdened and delighted by the influence and effect of using art to inform, encourage and empower the community. Thus far, SISTAAH has been notified by three community members (including one man) who reported that as a result of attending a SISTAAH arts event, they availed themselves of information, followed through with cancer screening and WERE DIAGNOSED EARLY as a result!

To all of those who are diagnosed with cancer, I urge you to get support! If you join a peer support group, you can obtain information and encouragement from those who have walked through that storm and who truly understand what you are going through.

To all of the people who are walking around with curable early stage disease, but will die because of inaction and fear — I am reminded of two slogans that I recite from time to time when I address groups about being proactive about their health.

"Your silence does not protect you." Audre Lorde

"You cannot conceal your illness and expect a cure." Ethiopian proverb

---

The daily stress and strain of performing a multitude of tasks often renders a woman drained of time and energy for self-care;

Her frame is pierced where chunks have been taken by those who constantly need a piece of her: family, neighbors, work, church, and community;

She stands upon a weather-worn backdrop of red, which signals crisis, but also courage and strength;

Her arms of stainless steel are strong, outstretched and constantly open in a posture ready for welcoming, embracing, loving, accepting, juggling duties and doing the impossible every day. She is a multi-tasking superwoman and, indeed, she can fly!

Her bosom has endured the surgical knife and she emerges victoriously;

She is perpetually standing at attention, her feet poised for action;

Even as she strategizes and makes plans, her curly, kempt tresses remind us that she values her beauty and appearance. Her face is the visage of any woman, every woman.

Many Woman is part of myself, and many mothers, grandmothers, aunts, sisters, cousins, neighbors and friends. Indeed, Many Woman is likely you.

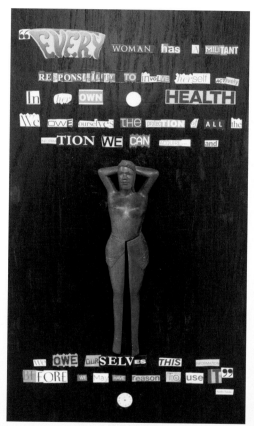

Every Woman Has a Militant Responsibility

Like *Many Woman* we tend to take care of others' needs before our own. But I can attest, with authority as former flight attendant, that it is absolutely true that you must put on your own oxygen mask first, then you will be able to assist another person. I hope that the information in this book will inspire others to think differently about wellness and become more proactive about their health. Regardless of what the health issue might be, it is best to address the problem before it goes out of control.

I urge people to begin thinking about engaging in art and experiencing the transformative and healing aspects of art-making. Whether it is singing, dancing, photography, writing, painting, drawing or sculpting, life is richer and more fulfilling if it includes art from the perspective of a participant rather than a spectator.

Over the years I have eagerly shared my story of hope and survivorship numerous times on television, on radio, in documentary films, in newspapers and in two anthologies. I have created my own book to help spread the early detection message and to document and honor my existence, my struggle, my journey, my survivorship, and my legacy. The way I see it, cancer did not erase anything from me, but instead, the series of events that have occurred after diagnosis have enriched my life. I continually get calls from people who have been newly diagnosed and were referred to me by friends or relatives who are familiar with me. Still others get in contact because they met me at an arts exhibition and are aware of my story. Many of those calls are requests to minister to those who are at the very beginning of their cancer journey and need suggestions as to where to go and what to do next. I am not an expert, but I do possess a wealth of information and resources. It is a privilege to share with others.

Art has enhanced my journey and has contributed immensely to my life in terms of experiencing fellowship, beauty and transformation. Art is magical! So here I stand with unwavering faith and optimism for a continuing, content, and creative future with a feeling of fullness!

I wish you good health, creativity and long life.

Lacking Nothing

RESOURCES

FACTS FOR LIFE

Breast Cancer Resources (Reprinted with Permission)

For more information, visit www.komen.org or call Susan G. Komen's breast care helpline at 1-877 GO KOMEN (1-877-465-6636) Monday through Friday, 9 AM to 10 PM ET.

This fact sheet lists resources that may help you. The Internet can provide breast cancer information as well. Make sure the information is reliable and trustworthy. Ask these questions: Is the source reputable? Is the source affiliated with a university, health organization or government agency? Before you take any action based on something you find on the Web, talk with your health care provider. Get at least one other opinion, then decide what is best for you. The list below includes suggested resources, but is not a complete listing of breast cancer organizations or information.

Organizations

Susan G. Komen® — promises to save lives and end breast cancer forever by empowering people, ensuring quality care for all and energizing science to find the cures. For information and support, call 1-877 GO KOMEN (1-877-465-6636), www.komen.org

American Cancer Society — provides medical information, treatment decision tools, news updates and support resources. 1-800-ACS-2345, www.cancer.org American Cancer Society Breast Cancer Facts and Figures 2015-2016 - http://www.cancer.org/acs/groups/content/@research/documents/document/acspc-046381.pdf

American Society of Clinical Oncology — has goals of improving cancer care and prevention and ensuring that all patients with cancer receive the highest quality care. 1-888-282-2552, www.asco.org

American Society of Plastic and Reconstructive Surgeons — advances quality care to plastic surgery patients by encouraging high standards of training, ethics, physician practice and research in plastic surgery. www.plasticsurgery.org

BreastCancerTrials.org — provides patient-centered information about breast cancer clinical trials. 415-476-5777, www.breastcancertrials.org

Facing Our Risk of Cancer Empowered, Inc. (FORCE) — provides information for women whose family history or genetic status puts them at high risk of ovarian and/or breast cancer. 1-866-288-RISK, www.facingourrisk.org

Fertile Hope — provides reproductive information, support and hope to cancer patients whose treatments present the risk of infertility. 1-866-965-7205, www.fertilehope.org

Food and Drug Administration Breast Implant Information — answers questions about breast implants. www.fda.gov

Inflammatory Breast Cancer Research Foundation — committed to finding the cause, focusing on research and awareness. 1-877-786-7422, www.ibcresearch.org

Living Beyond Breast Cancer — offers programs and services to women affected by breast cancer, caregivers and health care providers. 1-888-753-LBBC, www.lbbc.org

Mautner Project, The National Lesbian Health Organization — provides education, support and other services to lesbians with cancer. 1-866-MAUTNER, www.mautnerproject.org

Men Against Breast Cancer™ — leverages the important role of the husband/partner caring for the woman he loves. 1-866-547-MABC, www.menagainstbreastcancer.org

National Cancer Institute's Cancer Information Service — provides information and resources for patients, the public and health care providers. 1-800-4-CANCER, www.cancer.gov

National Comprehensive Cancer Network — improves the quality and effectiveness of care provided to patients with cancer. Offers clinical practice guidelines for patients. 1-866-788-NCCN, www.nccn.org

National Lymphedema Network — provides information on lymphedema. 1-800-541-3259, www.lymphnet.org

Nueva Vida — Spanish support network for Latinas with cancer. 1-866-986-8432, www.nueva-vida.org

Sisters Network, Inc. — provides outreach and education on the impact of breast cancer in the African American community. 1-713-781-0255, www.sistersnetworkinc.org

Triple Negative Breast Cancer Foundation — raises awareness of the disease while supporting research. 1-877-880-TNBC, www.tnbcfoundation.org

Young Survival Coalition® — provides information on breast cancer in young women. 1-877-972-1011, www.youngsurvival.org

Advocacy

National Breast Cancer Coalition — grassroots organization with a mission to eradicate breast cancer through action and advocacy. 1-800-622-2838, www.breastcancerdeadline2020.org

The Patient Advocate Foundation — provides legal and advocacy help with disputing insurance claim denials. 1-800-532-5274, www.patientadvocate.org

Support Programs and Services

American Cancer Society — visits newly diagnosed post-surgical patients by trained breast cancer survivors through their Reach to Recovery program. 1-800-ACS-2345, www.cancer.org

CancerCare® — provides free, professional support services to anyone affected by cancer. Services include counseling, education, financial assistance and practical help. 1-800-813-HOPE, www.cancercare.org

Cancer Support Community — ensures that all people impacted by cancer are empowered by knowledge, strengthened by action and sustained by community. 1-888-793-9355, www.cancersupportcommunity.org

Kids Konnected — provides friendship, understanding, education and support for kids and teens who have a parent with cancer or have lost a parent to cancer. Se Habla Espanol. 1-800-899-2866, www.kidskonnected.org

Living Beyond Breast Cancer — Find information on breast cancer support and care. 1-888-753-LBBC, www.lbbc.org

Financial Resources

There are many resources that may help with financial decisions. The first place that people can turn to for advice is a trusted health care provider. Doctors, nurses and social workers can all provide information and advice about financial questions. These resources may also help:

American Association of Retired Persons (AARP) — provides detailed information on a range of health issues for people over 50, including Medicare and other health insurance programs. 1-888-OUR-AARP (1-888-687-2277), www.aarp.org/health

CancerCare® Co-Payment Assistance Foundation —addresses the needs of individuals who cannot afford their insurance co-payments to cover the cost of medications for treating cancer. 1-866-55 COPAY, www.cancercarecopay.org

Cancer Financial Assistance Coalition — helps cancer patients manage their financial challenges. www.cancerfac.org

Corporate Angel Network — provides air transportation to treatment centers. 1-866-328-1313, www.corpangelnetwork.org

HealthWell Foundation® — reduces financial barriers to care for underinsured patients with chronic or life-altering diseases. 1-800-675-8416, www.healthwellfoundation.org

Healthcare.gov — provides information on finding insurance options, prevention and comparing the quality of health care providers.

Linking A.R.M.S.™ — offers qualified individuals financial assistance to help cover the costs of some treatment and medications, medical equipment including lymphedema support and supplies.

Linking A.R.M.S.™ is a partnership with Susan G. Komen® and CancerCare®. 1-877 GO KOMEN (465-6636) or 1-800-813-HOPE (4673), www.cancercare.org

National Breast and Cervical Cancer Early Detection Program — provides access to critical breast and cervical cancer screening services for underserved women in the United States. 1-800-CDC-INFO, www.cdc.gov/cancer/nbccedp

National Patient Air Travel HELPLINE — provides air transportation to treatment centers. 1-800-296-1217, www.patienttravel.org

Partnership for Prescription Assistance—provides information on how to find pharmaceutical manufacturer assistance programs. 1-888-4PPA-NOW, www.pparx.org

Patient Access Network Foundation — helps underinsured patients afford the co-payments for their cancer medications. 1-866-316-7263, www.panfoundation.org

Patient Advocate Foundation — offers a Co-Pay Relief Program that provides financial assistance to eligible patients who are being treated for breast cancer. 1-866-512-3861, www.copays.org

The National Financial Resources Guidebook for Patients — provides information state by state for financial relief for a broad range of needs including housing, utilities, food, transportation to medical treatment and children's resources. 1-800-532-5274, www.patientadvocate.org

YWCA — offers ENCOREplus® breast and cervical cancer program that provides outreach, education and screening mammograms to women who are most in need and lack access to breast health services. 202-467-0801 or contact your local YWCA. www.ywca.org

The above list of resources is only a suggested resource and is not a complete listing of breast cancer materials or information. The information contained herein is not meant to be used for self-diagnosis or to replace the services of a medical professional. Komen does not endorse, recommend or make any warranties or representations regarding the accuracy, completeness, timeliness, quality or non-infringement of any of the materials, products or information provided by the organizations referenced herein.

For more information, visit www.komen.org or call Susan G. Komen's breast care helpline at 1-877 GO KOMEN (1-877-465-6636) Monday through Friday, 9 AM to 10 PM ET.

Additional Resources

SHARE for Women Facing Breast or Ovarian Cancers

Provides telephone support, support groups, educational programs, and advocacy activities. Call toll-free (866) 891-2392 to talk to someone about breast or ovarian cancer -- in English, Spanish, and 10 other languages. HELPLINE: 844.ASK.SHARE (844.275.7427) or dial direct:

Breast Cancer: 212.382.2111
Ovarian Cancer: 212.719.1204
Ovarian Cancer toll-free: 866.537.4273
Espanol (seno y ovario): 212.719.4454

The Celebrating Life Foundation is a non-profit organization devoted to educating the African American community and women of color about the risk of breast cancer, to encouraging advancements in the early detection and treatment, and to improving survival rates among these women.

12100 Ford Road, Suite 100
Dallas, Texas 75234
www.celebratinglife.org
972-501-9981 ext 110

The Creative Center at University Settlement is a 501(c)(3) nonprofit organization dedicated to bringing the creative arts to people with cancer, chronic illnesses, and through all stages of life.

info@thecreativecenter.org
www.thecreativecenter.org
646-465-5313
646-465-5314

SISTAAH (Survivors Inspiring Sisters Through Art & Advocacy for Health, Inc.) (a sponsored project of Fractured Atlas). SISTAAH creates art events to encourage and facilitate access to early detection by informing medically underserved people of the availability of no-cost screening services.

Wilhelmina Grant 212-926-3517
www.wilhelminagrant.com
www.sistaah.org
SISTAAHstudio@gmail.com

Mo in the Mirror

MEET THE SISTAAH MASCOTS

Mo, the pigeon was left behind after a symbolic "White Dove" Release Ceremony which sent prayers, messages, wishes and dreams skyward during the annual *Survivorship Saturday in Harlem Celebration* in October 2012. Mo did not fly away with the other birds and was discovered hours later in front of the venue, pacing back and forth in the evening darkness atop the freshly fallen snow. I felt responsible for her safety and well-being, so I took her home. I later inquired at a pet shop about caring for my new houseguest. The sales clerk who sold me some bird seed and a cage reassured me that the bird would be okay. Without knowledge of the recent events, he exclaimed, "Don't worry, you can't hurt a pigeon — they are survivors." (Wow!)

Mo spends her days cage-free, fluttering her wings, munching on assorted seeds and grains, and strutting through the apartment. Her favorite pastimes are posing for photos and gazing at the pretty bird in the mirror.

A few months after Mo's arrival, Sandra, a rescued king pigeon whose leg was wounded when she was a squeaker, came to live with us. Sandra and Mo love to chase each other around, flap their wings and refresh themselves in a shallow bowl of water. After their splashy bath, they relax on a perch while their feathers dry.

Sandra and Mo

ART TITLES, DESCRIPTIONS AND PHOTO CREDITS

(ALL ARTWORKS BY WILHELMINA GRANT)

Time Into Eternity, 2015. (Front cover) Assemblage: broken clock, bookends, tie down, rusty chain, on wood, 18" x 48" Tribute to ancestors who battled breast cancer; photo: Zack Lewis

Churning Sea, 2015. Alcohol ink on ceramic tile, 12" x 12" photo: courtesy of the artist

It Takes a Village, ca. 1958. photo: courtesy of the artist

Chilling in the Engine, 1994. photo: courtesy of the artist

Solo Kata, 1994. photo: courtesy of the artist

When Life Gives You Lemons, 2010. Assemblage: earring, nails, construction mesh, nails on cutting board, 11" x 19" photo: Richard E. Conde

High Kick, 1994. photo: courtesy of the artist

Injustice and Inequality, 2010. Assemblage: found objects on cutting board, 15"x 20" photo: Richard E. Conde

Survivor, 2009. Assemblage: photograph, button, baby bottle nipple on cutting board, 13"x 17" headshot: George Ligon; art photo: Richard E. Conde

Discombobulated, 2009. Assemblage: cutlery drawer, nails, wire mesh, 13" x 19" photo: Richard E. Conde — Even under the best circumstances, it is often difficult to navigate the health care maze.

Fearless Fighting Spirit, 2010. Assemblage: photo, found objects on wood, 27" x 36" Acceptance of challenges, bouncing back and fighting cancer with both hands; photo: Richard E. Conde

Kicking Cancer to the Curb, 2010. Assemblage: infusion tubing, mannequin arm, found objects on wood, 22" x 24" — artist's visualization of each droplet of chemo drugs as a karate warriors punching and kicking cancer cells out – Photo: Richard E. Conde

Bald and Beautiful, 1994. photo: Zenobia Conkerite

Ocean Frolic, 1995. photo: courtesy of the artist

Eagle Eyed Grateful Lady, 2011. photo: Richard E. Conde

Less Diagnosis But More Death, 2008. Assemblage: baby bottle nipples, duct tape, scrabble tiles on wood, 24" x 40" photo: Richard E. Conde — According to The American Cancer Society statistics, Black women have the lowest survival rate of any racial or ethnic group. Poverty, less education, and a lack of health insurance are also associated with lower breast cancer survival. We need action to reduce that disparity.

Eliminate Cancer African-American Community Behind the 8-Ball, 2010. Assemblage: found objects on wood, 14"x13" photo: Richard E. Conde

Breasts, Bandages and Red Tape, 2008. Assemblage: baby bottle nipples, duct tape, scrabble tiles on cardboard, 36" x 28" photo: Richard E. Conde - Millions of U.S. dollars have been spent internationally on military aggression and other related expenditures. Meanwhile, the breast cancer cure remains forthcoming.

Girl Talk, 2008. Acrylic on paper, 14" x 11" photo: Richard E. Conde — One of a series of four bare-breasted pressure-prints of the artist. The presence of the removed breast is still experienced from time to time in the artist's psyche. The right breast states *"I miss you,"* and the left breast replies *"I miss you, too."*

Community College Graduation, 2004. photo: courtesy of the artist

Bachelor of Arts, 2006. photo: courtesy of the artist

Grace Under Pressure, 2015. Assemblage: rusty, flattened spray can, found jewelry, 10" x 13" photo: courtesy of the artist

Stamp Out Breast Cancer, 2010. Assemblage: scaffold nails, scrap metal, pendulum, gold leaf paint, 12" x 12" photo: Richard E. Conde

Do the Right Thing, Get a Mammogram, 2015. Assemblage: clock base, keys, found jewelry, 10" x 10" photo: Rudy Collins

Every Woman Has a Militant Responsibility, 2010. Assemblage: found objects on cutting board, "17 x 30" photo: Richard E. Conde

Tolerating the Hot Comb, 2009. Assemblage: steel wool, found metal, hot comb, found objects on wood, 10" x 18" photo: Richard E. Conde

Tolerating the Hot Comb-2, 2010. Assemblage: steel wool, found metal, hot comb, found objects on wood, 9" x 14" photo: Richard E. Conde

Hot Comb in the Kitchen, 2010. Assemblage: steel wool, found metal, hot comb, found objects on wood, 9"x14" photo: Richard E. Conde

Hot Comb in the Kitchen-2, 2012. Assemblage: steel wool, found metal, hot comb, found objects on wood, 12"x11" photo: courtesy of the artist

Dyed, Fried and Laid to the Side, 2015. Assemblage: hot comb, hair dressing tin, found metal on wood, 10" x 13" photo: Rudy Collins

Maternal Mortality/Shambled Eggs, 2010. Assemblage: clock, chip & dip bowl, umbrella shaft, lace, found objects, 24" x 50" photo: Richard E. Conde

Breast Portrait, 2010. Pastel on paper, art and photo: Clarity Haynes, *Radical Acceptance Exhibition and Catalog*

Graduate School, 2009. photo: courtesy of the artist

Fan Giveaway in the Park, 2013. photo: courtesy of the artist

2500 Fans, 2010. photo: courtesy of the artist

Many Woman, 2009. Assemblage: strainer, grater, salad knife, forks, found objects on wood, 18" x 24" photo: Richard E. Conde

Lacking Nothing, 2014. Assemblage: shoe horn, nails, found jewelry, 17" x 21" photo: Zack Lewis

Mo in the Mirror, 2012. photo: courtesy of the artist

Sandra and Mo, 2013. photo: courtesy of the artist

Artist headshot, courtesy of the artist

Front and back cover design: Deena Warner Design LLC

ABOUT THE AUTHOR

Wilhelmina Grant is a two-time survivor of breast cancer who accidentally discovered a lump in 1994, but almost went undiagnosed due to unconcern and misinformation on the part of the initial medical practitioner.

She is a self-taught visual artist who creates collages and assemblages using mixed-media and found objects which she repurposes into visual art. Many of the ideas that stimulate the creation of her work reflect her interpretations of contemporary social concerns: urban issues, anti-violence, and women's health matters with a focus on breast cancer awareness. Wilhelmina considers the transformation of outdated, rusty, or broken objects into art as a metaphor for personal growth, renewal and boundless possibilities. If life as a cancer survivor has given her lemons, then advocacy through art-making has truly become her "lemonade."

Wilhelmina has mounted 21 solo exhibitions in Harlem, Texas and Alaska, and has participated in 38 group exhibitions at venues throughout the New York area and the East Coast.

Wilhelmina has been honored with several prestigious awards for art, including *The Black Art Makers Award* of National Conference of Artists, *The Women's History Month Creative Power of Women Award* presented by New York State Senator Bill Perkins, *The Alain Locke Art & Action Award* presented by Harlem Arts Alliance, and *Woman of the Year* by the National Association of Negro Business and Professional Women's Clubs, Inc.

As an artist-in-residence, she nurtures the creativity of cancer patients, their families and staff in a hospital setting. She also guides elder participants through arts projects at senior centers in Harlem and Washington Heights.

Wilhelmina is the founder of SISTAAH, Inc. (Survivors Inspiring Sisters Through Art and Advocacy for Health), a non-profit organization which combines art with wellness advocacy. SISTAAH encourages and facilitates access to the early detection of cancer by informing medically underserved people about no-cost screening services.

Wilhelmina earned a Bachelor of Arts degree in English Language Arts (2006) and Master of Science in Urban Affairs (2009) from Hunter College. Wilhelmina, a native New Yorker, is a resident of Harlem, where she lives with two pigeons she adopted from a local wild bird rescue/rehabilitation group.

Printed in the United States
By Bookmasters